EVOLUTiON

Please visit our web site at: **www.garethstevens.com**
For a free color catalog describing Gareth Stevens Publishing's list of
high-quality books and multimedia programs, call 1-800-542-2595 (USA)
or 1-800-387-3178 (Canada). Gareth Stevens Publishing's fax: (414) 332-3567.

Library of Congress Cataloging-in-Publication Data

Change.
      Evolution.
           p. cm. — (Discovery Channel school science: the plant and animal
      kingdoms)
           Contents: Evolution—Giraffic park—A mammoth lumbering through the
ages—Extinction basics—It's a dog's world—Voyage of discovery—The Scopes
"Monkey" trial—Variation on a theme—The swamp thing—Begin at the
beginning—When whales walked—The case of the faulty fossil—Something
about Mary—Absolutely evolution—Save the icefish!
           ISBN 0-8368-3211-6 (lib. bdg.)
           1. Evolution (Biology)—Juvenile literature. [1. Evolution.] I. Title.
      II. Series.
QH367.1.C47 2002
576—dc21   2002023872

This edition first published in 2002 by
Gareth Stevens Publishing
A World Almanac Education Group Company
330 West Olive Street, Suite 100
Milwaukee, WI 53212 USA

Writers: Jackie Ball, Lynn Brunelle, Margaret Carruthers, Scott Ingram.

Editor: Lelia Mander.

Photographs: Cover, pp. 2 and 10, woolly mammoth,
© Jonathan Blair/CORBIS; p. 2, sloth, © Wolfgang Bayer/DCI;
p. 3, earth motif, MapArt; pp. 4-5, sloth, sloth in tree (both),
© Wolfgang Bayer/DCI; p. 6, giraffe, © Wolfgang Bayer/
DCI; p. 10, eagle, PhotoDisc; p. 11, earth motif, MapArt; p. 14,
Charles Darwin, © Brown Brothers, Ltd.; p. 15, *H.M.S. Beagle*,
© Bettmann/CORBIS; p. 15, compass, PhotoDisc; p. 16,
Clarence Darrow and William Jennings Bryan (both), Brown

This U.S. edition © 2002 by Gareth Stevens, Inc. First published in 2000 as
Change: The Evolution Files by Discovery Enterprises, LLC, Bethesda,
Maryland. © 2000 by Discovery Communications, Inc.

Further resources for students and educators available at
www.discoveryschool.com

Designed by Bill SMITH STUDIO
Project Editors: Justine Ciovacco, Lelia Mander, Sharon Yates, Anna Prokos
Designers: Nick Stone, Sonia Gauba, Bill Wilson, Darren D'Agostino,
  Joe Bartos, Dmitri Kushnirsky
Photo Editors: Jennifer Friel, Scott Haag
Art Buyers: Paula Radding, Marianne Tozzo
Gareth Stevens Editor: Alan Wachtel
Gareth Stevens Art Director: Tammy Gruenewald

Printed in the United States of America

1 2 3 4 5 6 7 8 9 06 05 04 03 02

Brothers, Ltd.; p. 17, John Scopes, © Hulton-Deutsch Collection/CORBIS;
p. 19, sand cat, © Terry Whittaker/Photo Researchers, Inc., pallas cat, © Tom
McHugh/Photo Researchers, Inc.; p. 21, fern fossil, © VU/Inga Spence; p. 22,
bacteria, Juergen Berger/Photo Researchers, Inc.; pp. 24-25,
whales, © 98 Amos Nachoum; pp. 28-29, Louis and Mary
Leakey, Robert Sisson/NGS Image Collection. All other
photos by Corel.

Illustrations: p. 8, Moeritherium and Phiomia, Alan Male;
p. 18, miacid, Alan Male; p. 24, wing, whale's fin, and human
arm, Christopher Burke.

DISCOVERY CHANNEL SCHOOL SCIENCE

CONTENTS

Life on Earth began about 3.5 billion years ago—some say even earlier. It started out as tiny, one-celled organisms that lived in the ocean. Then everything changed. Look around you—life is everywhere, in all shapes, sizes, and varieties. It's an amazing transformation.

How did it happen? How did one species eventually give rise to millions of others, of so many different kinds? For one thing, it happened over a very long time. But other forces were at work, too. Living beings all compete for the same limited supplies of food, and they all face similar hardships. Some species are better equipped to deal with these challenges than others. These species will thrive, while the others won't. It's not always a pleasant story, but it's the way evolution works.

Join Discovery Channel and EVOLUTION to find out how this process works. Explore the evidence and see the results. After all, you're a product of evolution, too.

EVOLUTION

Man's best friend?... See page 12

Final Project

Evolution

That creature hanging from that tree certainly looks comfortable. And why not? The three-toed sloth, whose scientific name is *Bradypus tridactylus*, sleeps about 20 hours a day, hanging upside down high in the leafy rain forest canopy. Actually, it might be hard to tell the difference between a sleeping sloth and one that's awake, since a sloth moves so sl-o-o-wly. You could walk 30 or 40 city blocks in the time it would take a sloth to cover just one.

So what does the slowest mammal in the world have to do with evolution, the process by which a species changes over time? Well, evolution is slow, too. It takes thousands, even millions, of years for species to evolve. Also, the sloth has survived, and survival through successful adaptation is what evolution is all about. Charles Darwin maintained, and the majority of scientists now believe, that members of a species with characteristics and behaviors that fit in best to their environment have the best chance of surviving—and therefore passing their traits on to the next generation. These characteristics and behaviors are called adaptations. The three-toed sloth has adaptations that help it live successfully in its rain forest environment.

Once, between 10,000 and 40,000 years ago, there were other kinds of sloths. Harlan's ground sloth, for example, was six feet tall, with powerful limbs and large claws. Sometime between then and now, this animal went extinct, along with many other large mammals. Scientists aren't sure what happened to them. Perhaps studying the adaptations of their closest living relatives will provide the clues needed to solve this ancient mystery.

MOUTH—The three-toed sloth is fussy about food, only eating the leaves, twigs, and buds from a certain kind of tree. What does this say about its ability to live outside the rain forest?

HEIGHT—*Bradypus tridactylus* is less than 2 feet (.6 m) long and weighs about 5.5 pounds (2.5 kg).

Slow but Safe

Even though "sloth" is another word for laziness, a sloth's pokey pace doesn't mean it's goofing off. Its lack of speed may be an adaptation; it could be protection against visual hunters such as eagles, which might spot a sudden quick movement more easily than a careful crawl.

ARMS—A sloth uses its long arms for defense and to pull itself hand-over-hand through the trees. Since its legs are too weak for walking, the three-toed sloth drags itself along by its hands on its once-a-week visit to the ground.

NECK—Nine vertebrae instead of the seven most mammals have enable the sloth to rotate its head in three-quarters of a circle.

FINGERS AND TOES—These are curved to hold onto tree limbs.

FUR—Long, coarse hair grows toward the ground and can shed rain. Beetles, mites, and moths live in the sloth's hair. So do green algae, which provide camouflage in the leafy treetops.

CLAWS—Three long, sharp, hooklike claws grip a branch so tightly that *Bradypus tridactylus* can sleep upside down and even stay suspended after it dies! Its claws are good for slashing at predators, too.

5

GIRAFFIC PARK

Q: You're a giraffe, the tallest land animal on Earth. Are we catching you at a bad time?

A: Not at all. I'm just doing what I usually do—nibbling leaves off tall treetops and looking down at the savanna with my big, beautiful brown eyes. Say, what's with the camera?

Q: We were hoping to get an on-air exclusive with you. We're from YOU ANIMAL, the program with a passion for the whole truth—no matter how nasty and damaging to anyone's reputation.

A: How noble. Thanks, but I think I'll just keep nibbling. But speaking of noble, why don't you go talk to that lion? He's good with the media.

Q: Maybe later. Right now we want to talk to you about a mysterious disappearance.

A: What disappearance? If you're looking for the leopard, she's over there. She's hard to see—or, hard to "spot." The pattern of her spots blends in with the pattern of light and shadow in the tall grass.

Q: Can we get serious here? We're on the trail of a short-necked giraffe that seems to have disappeared under very mysterious circumstances. We've heard you might know something about it.

A: Oh, I've known about the short-necks since I was a calf. It's part of every giraffe's family history. But it's history, not mystery.

Q: Are you sure?

A: Of course. You see, at one

time giraffes came in a greater variety of neck lengths, some much shorter than today's.

Q: Really? That must have been confusing.

A: Why? Red roses bloom next to pink ones, don't they? Within every living species, there's lots of room for variation, which comes from its genes. One of my ancestors, *Sivatherian*, looked more like a moose than a giraffe. It had longish horns, legs on the short side, and a much shorter neck.

Q: What happened to these other kinds?

A: They didn't survive. They couldn't compete.

Q: You mean there was a contest?

A: No, I'm talking about the ordinary, everyday competition that takes place in nature. Food supplies are limited, and animals have to compete for them—both with other species and within their own. The giraffes with the longest necks could reach leaves and twigs up high as well as the ones on the lower trees. The shorter-necks could only reach the lower-level food. As low vegetation disappeared, the longer-necks were better fed, and over generations that made them a bit stronger, healthier,

and better able to get away from predators.

Q: You're saying the short-necks starved?

A: Not exactly. But the stronger, healthier long-necks produced more and more young, and those babies had a better chance for survival because they were long-necked, too. Like their parents, they could reach more available food. The genes that produced long necks became more and more frequent with each generation. Nature wants a winner. It selects the qualities with the best chance of competing in an environment.

Q: So it's an entirely natural process? Not even a teeny bit of foul play?

A: It's entirely natural—that's why it's called natural selection. Short necks became rarer and rarer until eventually long necks replaced them. We were better adapted to our environment. My long neck is an adaptation. Want me to tell you about some others I have?

Q: Well, I guess we have to fill up our time with something, since there's no crime or scandal. Go ahead.

A: I have terrific eyesight, for one thing.

This, along with my height, lets me see a lion or any other predator coming so I can get away. My foot-long tongue can grasp leaves and twigs and pull them down into my mouth. Some of my teeth are grooved to strip the leaves away from the twigs. Oh, and my circulatory system is specially adapted for my long neck. I have elastic blood vessels in my head and neck to handle the changes in my blood pressure when I swing my head back and forth.

Q: And other animals in the savanna? Do they have adaptations, too?

A: Of course. You saw how the leopard's spots helped her become invisible to her prey. A zebra's stripes may help it blend into the herd so a predator can't pick out any one single animal. Adaptation is all about fitting in and meeting the challenges of the environment. That's the name of the game.

Q: Thank you, giraffe, for being on our show.

A: Happy to be a part of it— and that's no tall tale!

Activity

SAFARI TIME Do some research on other animals in the savanna. What did some of the zebra's ancestors look like? When and why did stripes become an adaptation? Or else, pick an animal in any environment and explain how it is adapted for survival.

A MAMMOTH LUMBERING THROUGH THE AGES

TIMELINE

Moeritherium

Phiomia

55 Million Years Ago (MYA)	40 MYA	30–15 MYA	11 MYA	4–5 MYA

HUMBLE BEGINNINGS

The oldest proboscidean fossils found so far are *Moeritherium*. This animal looks small and piglike. With its short legs, it only reaches about three feet (1 m) high, and it lives near the ocean shore. Instead of a trunk, it has an extended snout with a long, flexible lip at the end.

TRUNKS AND TUSKS

A trunk is an animal's nose and upper lip fused together and elongated. It allows animals to reach farther for food and water. Tusks can be used to strip bark off trees. They are also useful as a defense against predators. The first proboscidean to have a trunk and well-developed tusks is *Deinotherium*.

PROBOSCIDEA'S HEYDAY

Many different proboscidean species develop. Some have two tusks, some have as many as four. *Amebeledon*, for example, has a trunk and two upper tusks. Another cousin is *Phiomia*, which is about as tall as a horse. *Phiomia* has two short upper tusks. The mastodon also appears at this time.

THE FIRST TRUE ELEPHANTS

Unlike their ancestors, elephants have ridged teeth with thick enamel that are just right for grinding up grass. Other proboscideans, such as mastodons, eat softer leaves, so they don't need sturdy teeth. The first true elephants appear in Africa during this time.

STRAIGHT OR CURVED?

The elephant family splits into three species: *Loxodonta*, *Elephas*, and *Mammuthus*. The first two have straight tusks. *Mammuthus*, or mammoths, have curved tusks. For the first million years, all three live only in the tropics of Africa.

Woolly Mammoth

True or false?

Elephants are the direct descendants of woolly mammoths. The answer? False! It's true that both animals have long trunks and ivory tusks. And elephants are still around, while mammoths became extinct about 10,000 years ago. But mammoth fossils and the evolutionary record both indicate that mammoths and elephants are actually distant cousins that have an ancestor in common.

They all belong to the order of mammals called Proboscidea. This name comes from the Greek word *proboskis,* which means "method of providing food." In this case, it also refers to the nose or trunk. Let's take a closer look at this family tree.

2.5–3 MYA	1.5 MYA	250,000–100,000 Years Ago	12,000–10,000 Years Ago	Today
MAMMOTHS COME TO EUROPE	**MAMMOTHS MOVE INTO NORTH AMERICA**	**WELCOME THE WOOLLY MAMMOTH!**	**MASSIVE WIPEOUT**	**THE TWO SURVIVORS**
Some mammoths start migrating through the Middle East and Turkey, and then up into Northern Europe. These 10-ton (9.1 m. ton) creatures feed on bark, leaves, and fruit. Meanwhile, the mammoths in Africa disappear. Why? Either *all* mammoths have migrated into Europe and Asia by now, or those that stayed behind couldn't compete with elephants.	Earth is in the midst of an ice age! Much ocean water is frozen, making sea levels lower, and some land masses are now linked by dry land. One such link, Beringia, connects Asia with North America. Herds of mammoths migrate east to North America and quickly move south.	Cooler climates bring about the evolution of the woolly mammoth. Its shaggy, thick hair and 3-inch (7.6-cm) layer of fat help keep it warm. Its long, inward-curving tusks are useful for uncovering plants buried in the snow.	More than 100 mammal species die out, including the mammoths. Why? Temperatures have risen, affecting the vegetation. Perhaps many species are left with nothing to eat, or humans are hunting some mammals to extinction. Perhaps a new disease is to blame. There is evidence for and against each of these theories.	Only two of the once-large—160 species altogether—proboscidean family still exist: the African elephant (*Loxodonta africana*) and the Asian elephant (*Elephas maximus*). Frozen remains of a woolly mammoth have been found in Siberia. This find is a unique opportunity to learn more about proboscideans by studying actual organs and tissues, rather than just fossilized bones. Stay tuned!

Activity

FAST MOVERS? Mammoths only lived in Africa 3 million years ago. Yet fossils of 2.4-million-year-old mammoths have been found in England. How can you apply this information to figure out how fast the mammoths were migrating? Take the route described in this timeline, consult an atlas, and add up the distance between England and Africa. Use Lake Victoria, in central Africa, as your point of origin. If the mammoths were migrating at a consistent rate, calculate how fast they would be moving if the first ones reached England 2.4 million years ago. Also, estimate when they would have gotten to the areas that are now a) Turkey; b) Poland; c) Germany; and d) France. Then plot the distances and migration rates on a graph.

9

Extinction Basics

Evolution is a story of success, but also of failure. When a species fails to survive, we say it becomes extinct. This means it ceases to exist. It may have died out because its environment changed and it was no longer able to survive. Or, perhaps, new predators moved in and killed it off. Or, the species evolved into a new species that was better equipped to survive. Whichever way, once a species becomes extinct, there is no way to bring it back.

Words to Know

- A species whose population is decreasing is said to be **threatened**.
- A species whose population has decreased to a point that it may die out is **endangered**.
- A species that has disappeared from a certain area but exists in greatly diminished numbers in other areas is called **extirpated**.
- A species that no longer exists is **extinct**.
- The disappearance of between one-fourth and one-half of all life forms on Earth in an unusually short period of time is a **mass extinction**.

Downlisting is Good News

It may *sound* like a bad thing, but getting an endangered species "downlisted" is the goal of many environmentalists. The downlist is a list of animals or plants whose populations have stopped declining and have begun to increase. Some downlisted species include the American alligator, bald eagle, gray wolf, leopard, Arctic falcon, Virginia round-lead beech, and Maguire daisy

The Six Mass Extinctions in Earth's History

When	What Disappeared	Significance
435 million years ago, the end of the Ordovician Period	Tens of thousands of tiny plant and animal species living in the planet's one mega-ocean, totalling one-fourth to one-half of all life on Earth	Scientists believe that a planetary climate change led to the spread of glaciers. As seawater froze, the warm water in which most life existed disappeared.
360 million years ago, the Devonian Period	Mainly species living in the oceans, including coral builders and 70 percent of marine invertebrates. Plants and animals on land by this time weren't greatly affected.	Cause may have been a massive global cooling, similar to the Ordovician extinction, that killed off the warm-water life-forms in the oceans. Cooling could have started by glaciers forming on the major continent, Gondwana.
240 million years ago, the end of the Paleozoic Era	80 to 96 percent of all species, mainly ocean life	The largest mass extinction in Earth's prehistory.
205 million years ago, end of the Triassic Period	More than half of all reptiles and amphibians on Earth	This extinction led to the rise of dinosaurs, which became the dominant animals on Earth.
65 million years ago, end of the Cretaceous Period	All dinosaurs, most of the 100,000 species of plant life on the planet	This extinction may have been caused by a giant asteroid striking Earth. The impact may have thrown billions of tons of dust into the air, blocking out sunlight. No sun, no plants; no plants, no food for plant-eating dinosaurs; no plant-eaters, reduced food for meat-eating dinosaurs
Right now, according to scientists	About 3 species per day over the past century. Within the next 100 years, it is estimated that the average extinction rate will rise to 30 species per day.	The current extinction process is the only one in Earth's history caused by one species—humans.

How Many Species On Earth?

Between 10 and 13 million species may exist on Earth.
About 1.04 million of them are insects, plants, and vertebrates.

250,000 plant species

750,000 insect species

41,000 vertebrate species

- 4,000 mammal species
- 9,000 bird species
- 18,000 species of bony fish
- 6,000 reptile species
- 4,000 amphibian species

How Do Humans Cause Extinction?

One thing leads to another:

❶ Overkill by hunting and fishing → **leads to** → greatly reduced numbers

❷ Introduce → predators (rats) → competitors (cattle) → diseases (malaria) → **leads to** → new dangers to environments, especially in island habitats

→ **leads to** → "domino extinction" (if a species that is an important food source dies out, so do the species that live on it)

❸ Habitat destruction (rain forests) → **leads to** → much smaller natural environment → **leads to** → species isolated in too small an area and unable to migrate to areas with more food

❹ Burning fossil fuels → **leads to** → increased carbon dioxide in atmosphere and acid rain → **leads to** → global climate change; tropical life is most endangered

❺ Warfare → **leads to** → habitat destruction

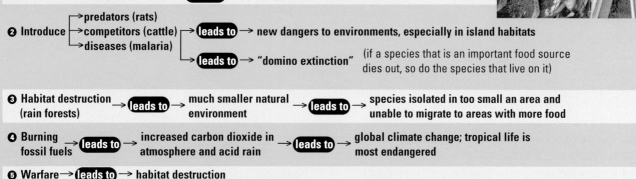

Rain Forests in Danger

Scientists estimate that, if rain forests in Central and South America continue to be destroyed by humans, in the next 100 years:

- 12 percent of 704 species of Amazon birds will become extinct.
- 15 percent of 92,000 species of South and Central American plants will become extinct.
- Estimated overall extinction rate: 17,500 species per year

Factoid: Scientists use the "species-area relationship" to estimate the number of species that will become extinct in a certain area. The relationship states that if a given area of wilderness is cut in half, 15 percent of the species living there will become extinct; if the remaining area is destroyed by half again, another 15 percent of species will be lost. For example, if 20 species live in one area, 3 species will become extinct when the area is cut in half.

Activity

DOING THE MATH Find out about the destruction of the rain forests in South and Central America. At what rate is this precious habitat being destroyed? How many species of plants and animals live in this region, and how many would be threatened? Obtain up-to-date figures from an unbiased source, and use the species-area relationship to make more projections on how many species will become extinct in the rain forests if current rates of habitat destruction continue for the next 50 years. Create a line graph to show the rates of extinction for insects, mammals, birds, trees, flowering plants, nonflowering plants, reptiles, and amphibians.

11

It's a Dog's World

Canis lupus, ancestor of all dogs

All the dogs on these pages are descended from one ancestor—*Canis lupus*, also known as the European wolf. If dogs came from wild wolves, how did they become man's best friend? And how is it that there are so many different breeds of dogs today?

Over 10,000 years ago, a hunter may have happened upon a wolf pup, which he brought back to his camp to eat later. Perhaps the pup did not ever develop its parents' aggressive behaviors. As the wolf grew up, it was adopted by the humans. Soon all the people in the tribe wanted a tame wolf of their own. Pups were captured from the wild. The ones with gentle, loyal natures were selected and kept. These wolves were then bred with other wolves owned by the tribe.

Over time and many generations, breeders have chosen the qualities they want in a dog, and they select dogs for these traits. This way the desired traits are passed on to the next dog generation, mimicing what happens in nature. In nature, however, the traits that get passed down are those that help a species survive best in its environment; human breeders' preferences have nothing to do with it.

When people breed animals to choose some traits over others, we call it artificial selection. These animals aren't being selected by the forces of nonhuman nature; it's not "natural" selection that creates a poodle or a pug. Instead, they're being selected by artificial means—by people's likes and dislikes.

This is how it works: Say you want a curly-haired, floppy-eared dog. In a litter of puppies, you choose only the dogs that have curly hair and floppy ears. When they grow up they are the ones allowed to mate—but only with other floppy-eared, curly-haired dogs. They produce mainly floppy-eared, curly-haired puppies. Over time, human beings have created hundreds of canine breeds, from Great Danes to Chihuahuas, and everything in between.

A wolf pup found in the wild by one of our hunting ancestors may have been the first example of "man's best friend."

Huskies are bred for their strength and stamina. Their thick fur protects them from the cold in the Arctic regions, where they pull supply sleds across great distances.

Dachshunds were originally bred to be low to the ground and have short hair so they could chase after hunters' quarries in bushy shrubs.

The sleek frames and thin bones of greyhounds give them speed for racing.

So-called "toy dogs," such as bichon frises and pugs, have been selected for qualities like size and shape of face.

Working dogs, such as German shepherds and sheepdogs, have been selected for their herding abilities.

Activity

SORT IT OUT Debate the pros and cons of artificial selection. Consider where else in the animal kingdom artificial selection is used.

13

Charles Darwin
1809-1882

Voyage of Discovery

Plymouth, England, Dec. 27, 1831

A 22-year-old naturalist named Charles Darwin packs his bags and is ready to head off on a journey around the world. He'll be away for five years. The ship, called the *H.M.S. Beagle*, is a research vessel, and Charles is joining the expedition as an unpaid observer. The living things and landscapes that Darwin would study, describe, and sketch in his notebooks would eventually change the way people look at nature and evolution.

H.M.S. Beagle, off Argentina, Oct. 2, 1832

The journey wasn't always pleasant for Darwin because he suffered from bad seasickness. For days on end, he stayed in his hammock, able to eat nothing but raisins. One solution was to go ashore whenever he got a chance. Once the *Beagle* reached the coast of South America, there were many opportunities. On firm ground, Darwin observed everything around him. What particularly interested him was the fact that some species lived in one place but not in another, even though the two places weren't that far apart.

In the morning we arrived at St. Fe. I was surprised to observe how great a change of climate a difference of only three degrees of latitude between this place and Buenos Ayres had caused … In the course of an hour I remarked half-a-dozen birds, which I had never seen at Buenos Ayres. Considering that there is no natural boundary between the two places, and that the character of the country is nearly similar, the difference was much greater than I should have expected.

Brazil, July 26, 1832

In Brazil, Darwin saw the biggest rodent he had ever seen in his life. In fact, it is the largest rodent species there is.

The largest gnawing animal in the world, the Hydrochaerus capybara *(the water-hog), is here also common … In the daytime they either lie among the aquatic plants, or openly feed on the turf plain. When viewed at a distance, from their manner of walking and colour they resemble pigs … As I approached nearer and nearer they frequently made their peculiar noise, which is a low abrupt grunt, not having much actual sound, but rather arising from the sudden expulsion of air: the only noise I know at all like it, is the first hoarse bark of a large dog. Having watched the four from almost within arm's length (and they me) for several minutes, they rushed into the water at full gallop with the greatest impetuosity, and emitted at the same time their bark.*

Galápagos Islands, Sept. 15, 1833

As he filled his journals with sketches and descriptions of new plants and animals, Darwin continued to be amazed by the huge diversity of life. Different versions of the same animals seemed perfectly suited to their varied environments. Was there a connection between them?

It was most striking to be surrounded by new birds, new reptiles, new shells, new insects, new plants, and yet by innumerable trifling details of structure, and even by the tones of voice and plumage of the birds, to have the temperate plains of Patagonia, or rather the hot dry deserts of Northern Chile, vividly brought before my eyes.

Survival of the Fittest

By the time Darwin was 37 years old, he had published several works on his observations. His work revealed several major questions about living things: Why was there so much variation? Why did different species compete to survive? Why did some species become extinct? Did some species change? And the largest question he had of all: What was the origin of these species? For years these questions haunted him, and the mystery of evolution remained elusive.

Then, in 1858, almost 30 years after his famous voyage, Darwin received a paper from a scientist named Alfred Russel Wallace. This paper contained many of the same theories that Darwin had considered. Just to see similar ideas in print helped Darwin put everything together. A year later he published his most famous work, *The Origin of Species.* Darwin put forth an amazing argument in this book. In nature, he claimed, there exists a huge variety of species and environments, and, in each environment, there is a life-and-death struggle for food and for the means to reproduce. Without eating and reproducing, no species can last into the future. And only the most fit of each species survives the struggle:

As many more individuals of each species are born than can possibly survive, and as consequently there is a frequently recurring struggle for existence, it follows that any being, if it vary in any manner profitable to itself, under the complex and sometimes varying conditions of life, will have a better chance of survival and thus be naturally selected. From the strong principle of inheritance, any selected variety will tend to propagate its new and modified form.

HMS BEAGLE

Activity

TAKING NOTES Darwin's work is based on his careful observations of plants, animals, and environments. Imagine that Darwin visited your neighborhood to study the plants, animals, and environment. Describe two animal species and two plant species as Darwin might have seen them, and try to give reasons for why they live where they live.

The Scopes "Monkey Trial"

Public Acts

OF THE STATE OF TENNESSEE

PASSED BY THE

SIXTY-FOURTH GENERAL ASSEMBLY

1925

CHAPTER NO. 27
House Bill No. 185

(By Mr. Butler)

AN ACT prohibiting the teaching of the Evolution Theory in all the Universities, Normals and all other public schools of Tennessee, which are supported in whole or in part by the public school funds of the State, and to provide penalties for the violations thereof.

Ad from the ACLU

The American Civil Liberties Union (ACLU, for short) considered Tennessee's law unconstitutional and decided to challenge it. The ACLU published this ad in newspapers across Tennessee:

We are looking for a Tennessee teacher who is willing to accept our services in testing this law in court.
—*Chattanooga Times*, May 4, 1925

A Football Coach Volunteers

When some townspeople in Dayton saw the ACLU's ad in the newspaper, they had an idea: Why not have the trial here? This "Trial of the Century" would make their little town famous. They decided that 24-year-old John Scopes, a high-school science teacher and football coach, was just the person to put the law to the test. The men explained the situation to Scopes, who happily agreed to be the defendant.

Spring 1925, Dayton, Tennessee

John Scopes, a science teacher in the local high school, has just been charged with teaching evolution to his students. He has violated a state law banning the teaching of evolution, or anything else that might contradict the biblical story of creation, in Tennessee public schools. Get ready for "the Trial of the Century!"

Scopes's trial was called the "Monkey Trial" because the theory of evolution claims that humans evolved from animals such as apes and monkeys. In the end, the "Monkey Trial" wasn't really about whether or not Scopes was guilty. It wasn't even about which of the two accounts of where humans came from is right. Instead, the trial was about whether or not Tennessee's law was constitutional. It was about making a distinction between science and religion. Most of all, it was about what we can teach and what we cannot teach.

Clarence Darrow (left) and William Jennings Bryan

Clarence Darrow in court

could or couldn't teach his students. In his opening statement, Darrow asked for a guilty verdict, saying "this case and this law will never be decided until it gets to a higher court, and it cannot get to a higher court probably, very well, unless you bring in a [guilty] verdict."

Dayton Has a Field Day

The citizens of Dayton prepared for thousands of visitors, hiring more policemen and arranging for additional guest accommodations. Someone even brought a couple of monkeys to wander around town. Other newspapers in the nation poked fun at Dayton for loving all this attention.

Outcome

The trial lasted for eight days. The jury delivered a guilty verdict, and Scopes agreed to pay the fine, although he made it plain that he believed the law was wrong: "I will continue in the future, as I have in the past, to oppose this law in any way I can. Any other action would be in violation of my ideal of academic freedom— that is, to teach the truth as guaranteed in our constitution of personal and religious freedom." Ultimately, the case went to the Tennessee Supreme Court and the verdict was overturned— on a technicality having to do with the fine. Tennessee's anti-evolution law wasn't repealed until 1967.

The Lawyers

As soon as William Jennings Bryan heard about Scopes's arrest, he quickly joined the prosecution. A well-known lawyer and congressman, Bryan was also a Christian with deep fundamentalist beliefs. In his view, the theory of evolution was a "bloody, brutal doctrine" that was an "attack upon the Christian religion." Clarence Darrow, a famous criminal lawyer, led the defense. He considered science important and supported teaching evolution. He also believed that it wasn't right for a state to tell a teacher what he

John T. Scopes

Activity

THEN AND NOW The issues surrounding the Scopes trial are still controversial today. Find a recent newspaper article on this subject and compare it to the Scopes case. In what ways have the arguments for and against teaching evolution changed, and how are they the same? Write a report of your observations. In one section describe the similarities, and in another explain the differences.

Variations on a Theme

Lynx

All cats are predators—even your sweet tabby. You can tell by their forward-facing eyes, plus by their sharp, flesh-tearing teeth and lean, muscular bodies. Cats have all evolved from a common ancestor, the miacid, which looked something like the modern pine marten. Today, you'll see an amazing variety of characteristics among the members of the cat family, depending on the environment in which each species lives.

Different environments have different challenges. For a cat to thrive in a certain place, it needs specific adaptations that give it an edge. Body size, fur color, pattern, and shape make a difference. After all, a cat living in the desert is going to have different needs than a cat living in the lush jungle or way above the timberline in the wintry mountains.

Rocky Mountains

❶

North America

Central America

❷

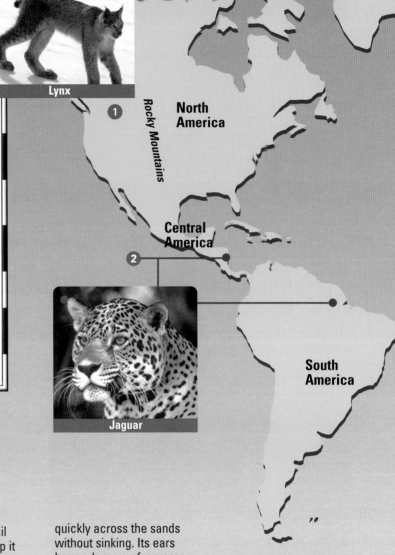
Jaguar

South America

The miacid is the common ancestor of all today's cats.

❶ The **lynx**, which lives in the Rocky Mountains in North America, has a short tail and tufted ears and feet. These features protect the animal from losing body heat during the icy winter months. The thick fur on its feet also acts as snowshoes, allowing the lynx to move across the snow.

❷ A **jaguar's** long tail and strong limbs keep it in balance as it navigates the tree branches of its rain forest environment. Equally at home in the trees and on the ground, this hunter's spots help it blend into the dappled sunlight of the forest. The jaguar can creep up on its prey without being noticed.

❸ The **sand cat** lives in the Sahara desert. It has tufted feet to protect it from burning sands and to allow it to move

quickly across the sands without sinking. Its ears have a large surface area for releasing heat, and they are also keen instruments for locating prey.

❹ Another African hunter is the **leopard**. This cat has developed the ability not only to climb trees but also to drag heavy kills up into trees after a hunt. A leopard can haul an antelope its own weight up into the high branches, away from other predators and scavengers.

❺ Long-legged **cheetahs** are the only cats without retractable claws. Similar to a dog's toenails, these claws give a cheetah great traction for its stunning bursts of speed. A cheetah will chase its victim until the prey is caught and knocked over. Then the cheetah grips its prey's throat with its powerful, clamping jaws and razor-sharp teeth.

Europe

Russia ⑨

Siberian Tiger

Pallas Cat

⑧

Himalayas

China

⑦

India

Sand Cat

Sahara

③

Snow Leopard

Africa

⑥

Lion

④

⑤

Australia

Leopard

Cheetahs

⑥ The African savanna is a sweeping grassland with many herds of animals and stealthy hunters. One of these, the African **lion**, has powerful muscles, a flexible spine, and sharp claws and teeth to help it catch its prey. Lions also blend into their tawny-colored environment and can get very close to their prey without being detected.

⑦ The thick, white fur with gray spots that hides a **snow leopard** in its snowy, high-altitude environment also keeps it warm. This cat has developed large lungs that help it breathe in as much oxygen as possible from the thin air of the Himalayas. Large feet give these cats a powerful base for leaping and an easy means of getting across the heavy snow.

⑧ The rare **Pallas cat** is perfectly adapted for life in the steppe—a vast, rocky grassland that stretches out across the southern part of Russia and into China. Its small body size and long, thick hair keep it warm in the winter and protect it from the burning sun in the summer. The Pallas has a flat head and eyes high on the skull. This eye position helps the cat peer over rocks in search of prey without being seen.

⑨ The **Siberian tiger** lives in the dense forest areas of Russia and northern China. Its stripes keep it disguised while hunting. As this predator moves through the woods, its stripes break up its silhouette among the shadows of the trees. The coloring of its coat also helps disguise the tiger at night.

The Swamp Thing

t is 325 million years ago, the end of the Carboniferous period. You are a *Lepidodendron* tree living in a warm, moist, tropical swamp. Rivers run nearby. Your upper branches tower 150 feet (46 m) above the swamp floor. Looking across the swamp to sandier, drier land, you watch tree ferns grow.

At the base of your trunk, patterned with diamond shapes, insects crawl about. A fishlike amphibian swims underwater, in between your roots. Up on land, your cousin *Sigillaria* grows. On the muddy banks are dense stands of giant horsetails, about 30 feet (9 m) tall. Every so often, the rivers flood, dumping sand and mud into the swamp and burying some of your old leaves and cones.

You are a strong tree, but you are getting old. Soon your leaves begin falling, you stop producing cones, and your branches begin to crack and fall off. One day, your entire trunk crashes into the swamp.

You've fallen into a foot (0.3 m) of water and onto a thick layer of dead leaves. Soon you will be part of a layer of peat that's 30 feet (9 m) thick, made of 30,000 years' worth of dead forest vegetation.

Life Underground

You lie in the swamp for thousands of years. As other plants die, you are slowly covered and buried. More and more plants pile on top of you. After a while you notice that you are all being covered in sand. What happened? Once you lived near a river, but now the sea is closer, and you are directly beneath a beach.

It's been millions of years since you've seen the light of day. You're being squashed by thousands of feet of sediments, and it is getting very hot. The water and air are slowly being squeezed out of you.

The deeper you are buried, the hotter it gets. Over millions of years, your cells turn black and brittle, and you are eventually not much more than a chunk of carbon. The 30-foot- (9-m-) thick peat layer you started in is now a layer of coal only three feet (1 m) thick.

What's become of your leaves, branches, cones, and roots? Over time, water has percolated through

Huge forces are at work underneath Earth's crust, and you are now being pushed back up, towards the surface, as part of a new mountain range. You can feel the layers above you eroding away. As rivers cut down into the rocks, the ancient layers are gradually exposed.

Seeing the Light

Air! Daylight! You never thought you'd see the Sun again, but, finally, you are out from under. It's the year 2002, and now you're in a much cooler, temperate forest in North America. You see some familiar things: small ferns and your cousins, the clubmosses, but there are no giant *Lepidodendrons*, no giant ferns, no *Sigillaria*, or giant horsetails. You are even more astonished to see plants and animals you have never seen before, such as beautiful dogwoods and other flowering trees, daffodils, and bluebells.

You hear a strange sound and notice a two-legged animal, covered in black soot, coming at you with a pick. He starts hacking away and throwing pieces of your coal in his wheelbarrow. A while later, you are sitting in a heap of coal in front of a fire. You thought it was over when your temperature was 392° F (200° C) and you were stuck several miles underground, but now it really looks like the end. You are picked up, and the two-legged creature is about to throw you into the fire when he notices your diamond pattern. He smiles, dusts you off, and carefully places you on the ground. Relieved to have escaped your final destruction, you look around. You're amazed to see that you are sitting among fossils of all of your old friends: a leaf impression of a fern, a *Sigillaria* bark impression in sandstone, tiny spores sitting under a microscope, a cast of horsetails, and your long-lost petrified branch. You realize that these small fossils are the only remains of your rich life in the swamp, all those millions of years ago.

some parts of them, replacing each cell with minerals. They have been turned into fossils. Some of your leaves, trapped in layers of sand and mud, have left detailed impressions. A cone was preserved in a ball of peat that somehow escaped turning into coal. It looks almost exactly like it did when it was alive.

Activity

FIRST IMPRESSION Find out more about the Carboniferous plants mentioned on these pages and examine clear, detailed drawings of them. They are usually shown in illustrated books about prehistoric life or the history of Earth. Then make your own sketch, as if you were the two-legged fossil finder in this story. Think about what information the fossils give you about the past and what they don't. Is there any way, for example, we can tell how tall a tree was by looking at a fossil of just a portion of its trunk?

BEGIN AT THE BEGINNING

Lynn Margulis, Ph.D., studies evolution on a microscopic scale. She's looking for clues to help solve one of the biggest mysteries in evolution: How did the very first one-celled organisms evolve into more complex life forms?

Some theories state that species evolved as a result of random gene changes. Genes, which are made of DNA, are what make individuals different from each other. If enough genes change, species change, too. Through many of these random gene changes, or mutations, new species would evolve.

Start by Asking a Question

Dr. Margulis wasn't convinced that this theory told the whole story. How could so many different forms of life have evolved randomly? She began her work by asking how the earliest life forms we know of—bacteria— evolved into organisms such as plants, animals, and algae.

In the course of her research, Dr. Margulis came across a radical theory: Maybe new species evolve by symbiosis. Symbiosis is when two organisms survive by living in close contact. Examples of symbiotic organisms

are all around us. Lichens, for example, are made of an alga and a fungus living together. Over many generations, Margulis thinks, some symbiotic organisms may have merged together and created a new life form.

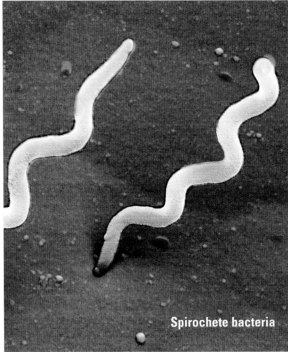
Spirochete bacteria

Bacteria vs. Everything Else

All living things are made of cells, but not all cells are the same. Plants, animals, fungi, and protists such as algae all have complex cells. These cells have special components, called *organelles*, that perform certain functions. Some organelles help cells use oxygen, and others, found only in plant cells, convert sunlight into food and oxygen.

Some cells have small tails, or cilia, attached to them, to help them move. Each of these more complex cells also has a nucleus, where most of its DNA is kept. Some DNA is also present in certain organelles.

Bacteria, on the other hand, are much less complex. A bacterium is always a one-celled organism, and this cell's structure is very simple. It contains no organelles or even a nucleus. Scientists have concluded that bacteria are the earliest life forms. At some point, bacteria must have evolved into more complex organisms. But *how*?

The different kinds of bacteria hold some clues. Some bacteria, such as archaebacteria, need extreme heat to survive and can't live in oxygen. Other kinds, such as cyanobacteria, breathe oxygen, or absorb sunlight and convert it to food. Still others, such as spirochetes, are shaped like long tails, and they move by switching their bodies rapidly from side to side. Could it be that some of the organelles in more complex cells began as bacteria like these?

Testing a Theory

Dr. Margulis proposed that complex cells may have evolved when bacteria came together through symbiosis. At first, they just lived closely together, but after many generations, they could have merged into a new life form. A swimming bacterium like a spirochete might have invaded an archaebacterium. The result could have been a one-celled swimmer that couldn't live in oxygen. Eventually, that species might merge with an oxygen-breathing bacterium, creating an organism that could swim and use oxygen to process its food. That organism then might eat a green bacterium, without digesting it. The final result could be a more complex life form—a swimming green alga!

The next step was to test her theory against the evidence. Dr. Margulis examined the DNA of various organelles and compared it to the DNA of different kinds of bacteria. She found that the DNA of a mitochondrion, which is an organelle that breathes oxygen in a complex cell, is very similar to the DNA of oxygen-breathing bacteria. She also learned that the DNA of chloroplasts, the organelles in plant cells that absorb sunlight, is very similar to the DNA of bacteria that also use sunlight.

She then compared cell tails, or cilia, to swimming bacteria, such as spirochetes. She found that though these may resemble each other in the ways they move, there is no DNA link between them. That's the nature of scientific research. Evidence comes in stages, and some quests are more elusive than others.

Is a Symbiotic Theory of Evolution "Right"?

For many years, biologists didn't accept Margulis's theory. Now, with such strong evidence, almost all biologists agree that she is, at least, partly right. Some parts of complex cells formed from bacteria that merged with simpler cells billions of years ago. But since we can't travel back to the time when this first happened, we may never know for certain. And there are other theories of how life evolved. The best we can do is keep our minds open and continue collecting evidence.

Take Notes!

All scientists record their observations in writing. This helps them keep track of what they have observed. It's also important for them to state their questions clearly. Here's what notes about Dr. Margulis's work might look like:

Question to Answer

How did simple bacteria evolve into complex plants and animals?

Interesting Observations

1. Symbiosis is everywhere.
2. The oldest fossils are bacteria (prokaryotes), about 3.5 billion years old.
3. According to the fossil record, complex cells (eukaryotes) didn't evolve until about 2 billion years later.
4. Some parts of complex cells look a lot like bacteria that are alive today:

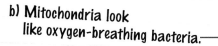

a) Chloroplasts (in plant cells) look like green, photosynthetic bacteria.

b) Mitochondria look like oxygen-breathing bacteria.

c) Cilia (cell tails) look like swimming bacteria called spirochaetes.

Activity

STEP BY STEP Write your own scientist's notebook, using Dr. Margulis's work as your topic. How would you write down the steps for the experiment and what you found out? Keep your information clearly labeled, and include a page indicating what conclusions you are able to draw based on the data collected from the experiments.

When Whales Walked

Whales, the biggest creatures on the planet, live in the sea, right? Sure, but it wasn't always this way. Fossils of whales show that these swimming mammals have been around for about 40 million years. They've been swimming in the oceans for a long time, but as long ago as 60 million years ago, the ancestors of whales were actually walking on land.

You would think that whales evolved from fish, since fish started out in the water. But the fact is that fish and whales aren't at all closely related. The reason evolutionists know this has to do with how fish and whales get their oxygen. Fish have gills that filter the oxygen out of the water. Whales have lungs and breathe oxygen from the air. Another clue is how each reproduces. Fish lay eggs and leave them to fend for themselves, while whales give birth to live babies and nurse them until they're ready to be on their own.

But, if their ancestors lived on land like most other mammals, then why did whales evolve to live in the water? Let's consider what the species needed to do in order to survive. It was competing with other mammal species for limited supplies of food, and it also needed to be safe from predators. At some point, a key change took place that improved the whales' ancestors' chances of surviving and producing future generations. For some reason, the four-legged mammal that lived by the shore began spending more and more time in the water.

Picture an animal with strong front legs, a tail, and long hind limbs. Scientists call it *Ambulocetus natans*, and it lived about 50 million years ago. It was about the size of a sea lion, and it may have moved on land in a way similar to the way sea lions move. It would have used its long tail and hind legs as paddles to move through the water. Maybe food was plentiful in the water and easier to catch. Perhaps the water provided this creature with a way to protect itself and escape predators. For whatever reason, over many generations, these seal-like walking whales took to the water. They became better swimmers and thrived.

Over millions and millions of years, their back legs started to get smaller, their tails morphed into flukes, and their front legs became flippers. Ten million years after *Ambulocetus natans*, a creature known as *Rodhocetus kasrani* evolved. The water made these ocean swimmers feel almost weightless. As time went on, they got larger and larger, since the ocean water could help them support heavier weights. Their hair became almost invisible and a layer of insulating fat grew in and protected these warm-blooded creatures from cold water.

The whales as we know them began to emerge and split into two groups. One group kept their teeth, though the teeth adapted to the hunting of fish and other sea creatures. These whales became dolphins, porpoises, orcas, and sperm whales. The other group feasted on the small krill that were plentiful everywhere. Their teeth slowly developed into sheets of hornlike mesh, called baleen, that were perfect for sifting their tiny food from the water. These whales became humpbacks, blue whales, and gray whales.

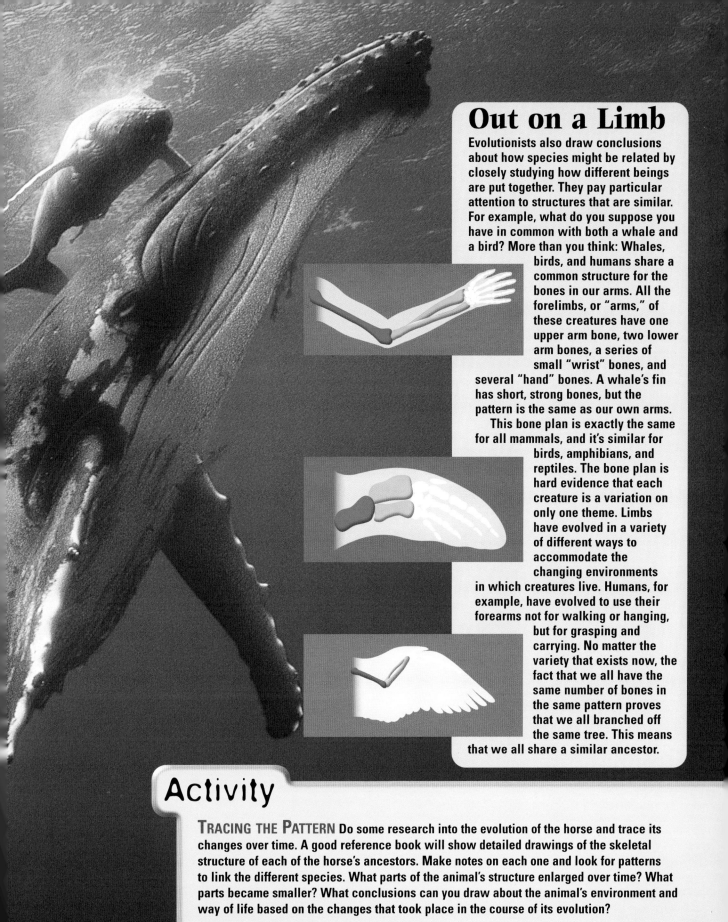

Out on a Limb

Evolutionists also draw conclusions about how species might be related by closely studying how different beings are put together. They pay particular attention to structures that are similar. For example, what do you suppose you have in common with both a whale and a bird? More than you think: Whales, birds, and humans share a common structure for the bones in our arms. All the forelimbs, or "arms," of these creatures have one upper arm bone, two lower arm bones, a series of small "wrist" bones, and several "hand" bones. A whale's fin has short, strong bones, but the pattern is the same as our own arms.

This bone plan is exactly the same for all mammals, and it's similar for birds, amphibians, and reptiles. The bone plan is hard evidence that each creature is a variation on only one theme. Limbs have evolved in a variety of different ways to accommodate the changing environments in which creatures live. Humans, for example, have evolved to use their forearms not for walking or hanging, but for grasping and carrying. No matter the variety that exists now, the fact that we all have the same number of bones in the same pattern proves that we all branched off the same tree. This means that we all share a similar ancestor.

Activity

TRACING THE PATTERN Do some research into the evolution of the horse and trace its changes over time. A good reference book will show detailed drawings of the skeletal structure of each of the horse's ancestors. Make notes on each one and look for patterns to link the different species. What parts of the animal's structure enlarged over time? What parts became smaller? What conclusions can you draw about the animal's environment and way of life based on the changes that took place in the course of its evolution?

The Case of the Faulty Fossil

Dr. Sophie Tarsier sat down with her morning mail. On top of the pile was a postcard from Randy Sykes, a former graduate student who had worked with her on a major fossil dig several years ago. The postcard was sent from the same mountain range where this excavation had taken place. Randy's exciting news nearly made Dr. Tarsier spill her cup of coffee. His note read:

THE AGE OF REPTILES

Dear Sophie—

I'm back in this beautiful area for some camping and hiking. I pitched my tent near Glacier Lake, and one day I was down at the stream, getting some water. You won't believe what I found—the fossilized remains of an ancient bird! Big deal—you of all people know there are tons of bird fossils up here. But this one was in a layer of sandstone, which was lying underneath a layer of coal!

Doesn't this prove that birds evolved before reptiles? There's no question that the coal is from the Carboniferous Period, about 320 million years ago. But the coal layer is on top of the sandstone, so the sandstone layer must be older. This means the bird remains are older, too! Can you believe that birds evolved 350 million years ago??

Gotta run. I'll give you a call as soon as I get back in town.

Randy

Dr. Tarsier is a paleontologist who specializes in bird evolution. All of her research convinced her that birds descended from dinosaurs. Randy's discovery might prove that birds were around *way* before dinosaurs—a full 200 million years earlier than was previously thought.

She reread the postcard and confirmed that Randy had done his homework. He was certainly using the Law of Superposition correctly, as she had taught him, to determine the relative ages of sedimentary and volcanic rocks. "Superpose" simply means "lie on top of." This law states that younger rocks lie on top of older rocks, and geologists have been using it for the past 200 years to decide whether one set of fossils is older or younger than another set. According to this rule, the bird would have to be older than the coal layer because it was found below the coal. The sand was deposited first, and then the coal.

Randy's discovery could force paleontologists to reconsider everything they thought about the evolution of birds. The evolutionary tree would have to be redrawn to put birds before dinosaurs—and even before reptiles.

Although she had nothing against new discoveries and theories, Dr. Tarsier was bothered by Randy's note. She remembered him well from the expedition. He was a bright student, but sometimes he rushed to conclusions before taking all aspects of the evidence into account. On the other hand, she didn't want to judge his work prematurely. She knew it was important to put the evidence before her own notions.

Dr. Tarsier got out her topographic and geological maps of the mountain range where Randy found his fossil. The maps showed a layer of coal and a layer of sandstone right near Randy's campsite. The coal layer was marked "Carboniferous Period: 320 million years old" and the sandstone layer was marked "Tertiary Period: 60 million years old."

The map showed that the sandstone layer was much younger than Randy believed. If it really was 60 million years old, then it was no surprise that bird skeletons were found there. On the other hand, the map clearly indicated that the sandstone layer was beneath the coal layer. Dr. Tarsier examined the map more closely. After a few minutes, she smiled. She'd figured it out. She sat down to write Randy a quick note.

What did Dr. Tarsier's note to Randy say?

Use these clues to help solve the mystery...

Clues

1. Not all rocks follow the Law of Superposition. Igneous rocks such as granites, for example, can push up from beneath or in between layers of rocks. A younger layer of basalt can actually lie beneath an older layer of sandstone.

2. Forces beneath Earth's crust can break and fold rocks. Layers can be tilted, turned upside down, or piled up on top of each other during mountain building.

Answers on page 32

UGANDA
KENYA
• Nairobi
Mombasa •
TANZANIA
Dar es Salaam •
Lake Tanganyika
MALAWI
ZAMBIA

Something about Mary

Tanzania, Africa, 1978

The blistering sun pounds the dry, sandy soil, and beads of sweat dry up before they can even drip off the faces and bodies of the workers. They are covered with dirt, and the salt from their sweat shows white and chalky on their faces. Digging, digging, digging. Using tiny trowels and brushes, the workers painstakingly sift through the sands. The work seems relentless and fruitless, but Mary Leakey holds firm. She has a feeling that this place where volcanic ash fell to the ground millions of years ago holds a clue, a piece of the puzzle.

But under the pounding sun and in the dirt and the dust, even she is beginning to have doubts. Then, suddenly, someone gasps. Silence hangs in the afternoon heat. Brushing away the African soil that had been undisturbed for 3.6 million years, Mary Leakey reveals a single footprint— a human-like footprint! There is a heel impression, an arch, a ball of a foot, and five toes.

Over the next few years, workers revealed two sets of footprints—one set smaller than the other and the two sets running less than a meter apart—with over 50 impressions in all. From the impressions, Mary Leakey and her team could draw many conclusions. They established that the living things that made the prints not only walked on two legs, but walked upright. Plus they walked this way all the time, not just occasionally, such as when running to escape danger. Most important, it was clear that these creatures were hominids, or members of the family Hominidae, the group that includes the great apes and humans.

The discovery that hominids were walking upright as long as 3.6 million years ago rocked the scientific world. This was much, much earlier than most anthropologists believed human's ancestors began walking upright. Leakey's remarkable discovery meant that our family tree had even deeper roots.

How might these prints have been made? Perhaps one day, 3.6 million years ago, two of our ancestors made their way across a field freshly covered with volcanic ash. Over time, the ash hardened and preserved their footprints. Then layers of dirt and sand collected over the hardened ash, leaving footprints from which scientists could estimate the height and weight of the beings that made them. By studying the depth and shape of the impressions the feet made, they could figure out how the creatures' legs and hip joints fit together.

But all of this was just business as usual for Mary Leakey, just another startling discovery in an amazing career that changed the way we look at human evolution.

All In the Family

Digging in the dirt was nothing new to Mary or her family. For decades, she and her husband, Louis, led excavations in Olduvai Gorge in Tanzania. While they dug in the African dirt, they sifted through the sands of time. They brought their son, Richard, along, and soon he, too, joined the family profession.

Over the years, the Leakeys made dramatic

Fabulous Fossil Findings

The Leakeys unearthed tons of evidence about our ancestors. Here are a few highlights:

- **1935–59** The Leakeys uncover many artifacts relating to Stone Age culture. They discover stone tools—axes, spearheads, and knives—that date from 100,000 to 2 million years ago.

- **1948** Discovery of the *Proconsul africanus* skull—the first fossil ape skull ever found. It is 18 million years old.

- **1959** Discovery of *Australopithecus boisei*, also known as *zinjanthropus*. About 1.75 million years old.

- **1960** Discovery of *Homo habilis*, the first toolmaker. The Leakeys also found hand bones that gave evidence that *Homo habilis* had opposable thumbs and a skull.

- **1965** One-million-year-old *Homo erectus* skull found.

- **1972** Fossil excavations reveal 15 previously unknown hominid species, some as much as 3.75 million years old.

- **1978–81** Footprints discovered that show that hominids walked upright as long as 3.6 million years ago.

discoveries uncovering fossil evidence of early primitive hominids. Their fossil findings dated back to as early as 18 million years ago, when, in 1948, they discovered the skull of the hominid *Proconsul africanus*. This was a human ancestor that, for a time, many people believed was the "missing link," or the species thought to connect humans with apes. The Leakeys' findings confirmed that our origins began in Africa and much earlier than originally thought. The fossils and tools they found showed a new picture of our family tree.

Among other things, the Leakeys' discoveries have unearthed a variety of hominid fossils, all dated to about the same time. Careful study of this evidence indicates that instead of a simple line of ancestors—one species evolving to another and, finally, to us—human evolution is actually a branching tree. At one point in our history, there were several different species of hominids, all living at the same time and competing against each other.

Thanks to the Leakeys, who are known today as the first family of paleontology and anthropology, we know a lot more about our human family tree. Not only is the human family older than we thought, but it is bigger and more complex. Through their fossil discoveries, Mary Leakey and her family have helped untangle the human family tree's branches.

Activity

THUMBS DOWN! A key adaptation that humans share with the great apes is the opposable thumb. This feature allows us to pick up and handle objects. Take a look at your own thumb. Notice how it has its own joint, located on a different part of your hand. Move your thumb back and forth and notice how it rotates at a distinctly different angle from your other fingers.

What would life be like without your opposable thumb? Put a rubber band around your right hand (or your left, if you are left-handed) so your thumb is tucked in towards your palm. Then try using your hand for various everyday activities, such as picking up a pencil, writing or drawing, opening a door, eating with a utensil, typing on a computer, turning on and off appliances, using a telephone, brushing your hair or teeth, and so forth. After removing the rubber band, make a list of activities you could still do without using your thumb and those that were impossible without it.

ABSOLUTELY EVOLUTION

"Don't Pull MY Leg!"

Whose family is it? A fossil leg bone has just been uncovered, and no one is sure from whose ancestor it came. It could be from any of the following: a horse, a dog, a bird, a human, an insect, a fish, or a bat. Look at the following clues to decide whose bone it is.

1 It's an animal with a backbone.

2 It's warm-blooded.

3 It's a mammal.

4 It doesn't fly.

5 It's a predator.

6 It walks on four legs.

Which Came First?

Put the following life forms in their correct sequence of origin on the evolutionary timeline, from earliest to most recent:

Reptiles   Dragonflies   Jellyfish   FERNS

Trilobites   Green algae   HUMANS   BIRDS

TYRANNOSAURUS REX   Big cats

Answers on page 32

30

Classification Clue

All living things on Earth are organized according to this classification system, designed in 1735 by Carl Linnaeus, a Swedish naturalist. There are seven categories, from the broadest (kingdom) to the most specific (species). The first and last may be easy to remember, but what about the ones in between? Here's a way to get the order right every time:

Kingdom	**K**ing
Phylum	**P**hillip
Class	**C**ame
Order	**O**ver
Family	**F**rom
Genus	**G**reen
Species	**S**treet

Why didn't the 2 million-year-old skull have teeth?

It forgot to floss—it!

Why did the female seal choose the big strong seal over the scrawny one?

Natural seal-ection.

Do you know *The Origin of Species?*

I don't know, can you hominid a few bars?

How many evolutionists does it take to change a light bulb?

One, but it will take at least a million years.

IT'S ALIVE!

Because their basic body plans haven't changed for millions of years, these organisms are called living fossils.

- **SHARK:** first slashed through the ocean waters 100 million years ago
- **COCKROACH:** first appeared in the nooks and crannies 250 to 400 million years ago
- **HORSESHOE CRAB:** found crawling the ocean floor about 430 million years ago
- **FERNS:** sprouted on Earth about 380 million years ago
- **TUATARA:** began creeping among the rocks 250 million years ago

KISSIN' COUSINS

The elephant is the largest mammal on land and is unlike any other animal on earth. Would you believe that its closest relative is the hyrax? This rabbit-sized mammal doesn't look a thing like an elephant, but they share some traits: they're vegetarians, their long incisors grow throughout their lives, and there are remarkable similarities not only in their foot bones but also in their DNA.

Hold-outs from the Past

What do you have that snakes don't? Legs, for one thing. A snake moves forward by wriggling its spine so its body shifts from side to side. But at one point in their evolution, snakes did have legs. Pythons still have tiny hip and leg bones—evidence of a leggy ancestor. Python legs and hips are vestigial—remnants of functional structures that have decreased in size over time. We have a vestigial structure, too—our appendix, which is a dead-end pouch on our intestine. A long time ago, we needed this feature to store food. Nowadays, it's more of a nuisance. But you can't expect these things to disappear overnight.

Save the Icefish!

Sometimes the most seemingly barren places on Earth are the best environments for certain life-forms to thrive and evolve into many diverse species. This is the case for the sea around Antarctica. These icy waters are home to a family of fish known, scientifically speaking, as notothenioids (no-toe-thin-EE-oids), that includes at least 94 different species. Some of these species are known as icefish because they are so pale. They are pale because their blood has no red blood cells to keep it from getting too thick in cold temperatures. Several factors have helped this fish family thrive:

One: The varied habitat of the Antarctic ocean environment includes deep ice canyons, sponge beds on the ocean floor (the Antarctic versions of coral reefs), and shallow areas.

Two: The cold waters make sure the fish have the place to themselves and don't have to share their environment with lots of other kinds of organisms that might be competitors for food or predators.

Three: Special adaptations, such as "antifreeze" proteins in their bodies keep their fluids from freezing. Notothenioids also overcame an evolutionary disadvantage. They started out as bottom-dwelling fish and, as a result, lost their swim bladder, a feature that helps a fish float to the water's surface. But in colder waters, the bottom was no longer the best place to be. To compensate, some of these fish developed layers of fat that are lighter than water and help them float. Others evolved lighter skeletons and scales.

Notothenioids are so well adapted, in fact, that any changes to their environment would suddenly threaten their survival. You've read about global warming and the melting of the Antarctic ice shelf. What if these trends continue? Should you save the notothenioids? Why? How would you go about it? Work with your classmates and come up with a plan. Consider the following questions as you put your solution together:

1. Describe the "worst case scenario" in detail. What are the challenges you would face? What are the consequences of the notothenioids extinction for the rest of the world?

2. Should the fish be saved, or should you allow natural selection to take its course?

3. Would it be feasible to "rescue" some of these species by moving them to an artificial environment? If so, how would you select which species would go?

4. Design some adaptations the notothenioids would need to survive such a change in their environment. How might these come about?

ANSWERS

Solve-It-Yourself Mystery, page 26:

Dr. Tarsier explained to Randy that, in fact, his bird fossil wasn't as old as 350 million years. The layers of sedimentary rock in his field area had been folded and faulted when the mountains were forming. The coal formed first, and the sandstone formed much later. Originally, the sandstone was on top of the coal. During mountain building, one of two things could have happened: Either the coal and sandstone layers were folded to such an extent that they were turned upside down, or the coal layer was pushed up on top of the sandstone along a fault. But in either case, the map was correct and Randy was wrong. The bird fossil and the sandstone layer in which it was found were both much younger than the layer of coal, even though the coal was on top.

Fun & Fantastic, pages 30–31
"Don't Pull MY Leg!"
The leg bone belongs to a dog.

Which Came First?
The correct sequence is green algae, jellyfish, trilobites, ferns, dragonflies, reptiles, *Tyrannosaurus rex*, birds, big cats, and humans